for Ramona

This edition published 2008 by Walker Books Ltd
87 Vauxhall Walk, London SE11 5HJ
10 9 8 7 6 5 4 3 2 1
© 1986, 2008 Jan Pieńkowski

The moral rights of the author/illustrator
have been asserted
Lettering by Caroline Austin

Printed in China

British Library Cataloguing in Publication Data is available
ISBN 978-1-4063-1432-8
www.walkerbooks.co.uk

WALKER BOOKS
AND SUBSIDIARIES
LONDON · BOSTON · SYDNEY · AUCKLAND

FACES

Jan Pieńkowski

happy

sad

angry

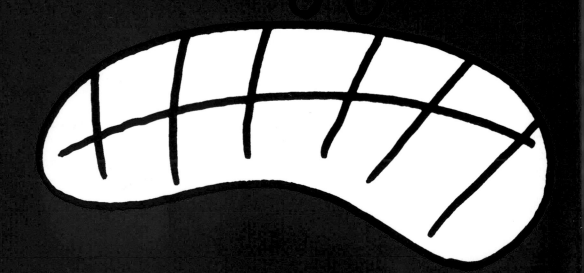

tired

shy

cheeky

jealous

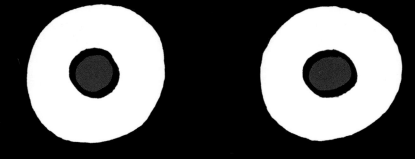

scared

proud

brave

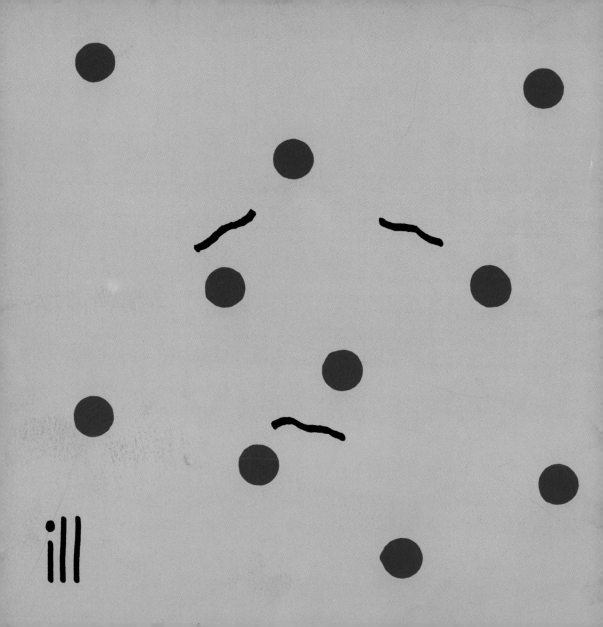